HR-Approved Way to Say the Things You Can't Say Out Loud at Work

By Still M. Ployed

Pebble Brook Press

This book is for entertainment purposes only. No HR Professional was involved in the making of this book.

If you enjoy this book, please consider taking a moment to leave a review on amazon.com. Thank you!

To the brave souls navigating the corporate jungle, may your coffee be strong and your meetings short.

TABLE OF CONTENTS

★

The Subtle Art of Not Losing It At Work

Ever found yourself politely smiling through a meeting that could have been an email, or nodding along to "constructive feedback" that was neither constructive nor helpful? Welcome to **HR Approved Way to Say the Things You Can't Say Out Loud At Work** - your trusty pal for navigating office life without losing your cool (or your job).

This isn't your typical career advice book; it's more like an unofficial survival kit. Here, we'll uncover the art of saying what you really mean in a way that won't land you in hot water—because let's be honest, "That's a terrible idea" sounds a lot better as "That's an interesting perspective; let's explore some alternatives". After all, the real trick isn't just about what you say; it's about how you say it.

User Discretion Advised

Use these gems wisely. While they may be HR-Approved, not all cubicle dwellers are Humor-Approved.

Chapter 1

FEEDBACK
Kind words for Tough Truths

> 🔍 How do I professionally say your idea sucks! 🎤

Your idea sucks! How did you even come up with something like this?

"That is an interesting angle. Let's explore some alternative approaches as well."

"You're not the expert here, I am."

"Based on my experience and background, I believe this approach will yield the best results."

"You constantly change things at the last minute and it's exhausting."

"To ensure smoother workflows, it would be helpful to finalize decisions earlier in the process."

———————————— 〟 —

"You take credit for my ideas, and it's getting old."

"I appreciate our collaborative efforts and would like to ensure my contributions are accurately represented in the future."

— 〝 ———————————

"I'm not a miracle worker!"

"This is an ambitious target—I'll do my best, but we may need to adjust the timeline."

"This feedback contradicts what you said last week."

I noticed a shift in direction from our last conversation—can we clarify the new expectations?

"I've explained this 10 times already."

"I believe we've covered this in our previous discussions, but I'm happy to clarify anything further."

——————————  —

"Your feedback is vague and not helpful."

"Could you provide more specific examples to help me better understand the issue at hand?"

— 66 ——————————

"If you're so picky about how this is done, why don't you do it yourself?"

"Since you have a clear vision for this, perhaps you'd like to take the lead?"

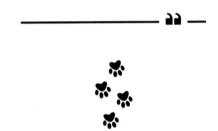

"This isn't my responsibility, but I'm always stuck doing it."

"I've noticed I've taken on some tasks outside of my role. I'd appreciate clarification on what is expected moving forward."

"I can't believe you thought that would work."

"It's an unexpected direction—can you walk me through your thought process?"

—— 〃 —

"I've had enough of your constant interruptions."

"To stay focused on the task at hand, it would be helpful if we could address all questions in one go."

— 〃 ——

"Are you serious with this request?"

"This is an interesting request! Could we discuss the feasibility further before moving forward?"

———————— 🙶 —

"That's not how this works, and you're making my life harder."

"For smoother execution, I'd recommend following the established process to avoid potential challenges."

— 🙶 ————————

"You're way off track here."

"It seems we've diverged from the initial goal. Let's refocus to stay aligned with our objectives."

———————— 🙶 —

"I'm tired of cleaning up your mess."

"I've had to make some revisions to your work. In the future, I'd appreciate it if we could double-check before submission."

— 🙶 ————————

"You're overthinking this, just make a decision."

"I believe we have enough information to make a confident decision and move forward."

———————————— 🙶 —

"I can't drop everything to prioritize this."

"I'd be happy to prioritize this, but I'll need to shift a few things around— could you help me reprioritize?"

— 🙶 ————————————

"You don't contribute anything to these meetings."

"I'd love to hear more of your insights during our discussions—they're valuable to the team."

———————— —

"This is way beyond my job description."

"This seems outside my current scope, but I'd be happy to assist where I can after completing my tasks."

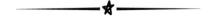

Chapter 2

EMAILS, EMAILS

and more emails...

🔍 How do I ask someone to stop flooding my inbox

"You're taking forever to get back to me. Are you even alive?"

"I'd appreciate an update when you have a chance, as this is time-sensitive."

—————————— 🙶 —

"You're flooding my inbox!"

"Would it be possible to consolidate these updates into a single email to make it easier to track?"

— 🙶 ——————————

"You sent this to the wrong person, again."

"I believe this would be best directed to [Insert Name], as they handle this area."

———————— 🙶 —

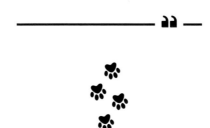

"I don't want to be on this thread."

"Feel free to exclude me if I'm not needed in future discussions."

— 🙶 ————————

"Stop copying everyone on these pointless emails."

"To keep things streamlined, let's limit the recipients to those directly involved."

——————————— 🙶 —

"Please stop emailing me after hours!"

"Just a heads-up - I'm on email duty from 9 AM to 5 PM, so I'll respond as soon as I can then."

— 🙶 ———————————

"I've explained this already. Twice."

"Please refer to the email I sent previously where this was addressed".

———————— 🐾 —

"I have no idea what you're asking for."

"Could you please provide a bit more clarity on your request to ensure I fully understand."

— 🐾 ————————

"Can you stop sending me chain emails?"

"Let's keep our email conversations lean and mean—just the highlights, please!"

———————————— 🙶 —

"That wasn't what I asked in my mail"

"Thank you for your thoughts! Could you elaborate on how this aligns with my request?"

— 🙶 ————————————

"Oh, another update... for attention?"

Thanks for the insight! It seems like everyone's got things covered—feel free to only share critical updates.

"This mail is totally irrelevant."

"This doesn't seem directly related to our current priorities, but thanks for sharing."

"I'm so done with these pointless updates."

"Thanks for sharing! A quick recap of the most important details would really help.

———————— 🙶 —

"I don't know why you copied me on this."

"Thanks for keeping me in the loop! Do you need any input from my end on this?"

— 🙶 ——————

"Why in the world is this mail classified urgent?!"

"This doesn't appear to be time-sensitive. Can we schedule it for later?"

————————————  —

"I'm totally ignoring this mail!"

"Noted! Please let me know if there's any immediate action required on my end."

— 66 ————————————

"I don't need to be involved in this at all."

"I trust you've got this covered! Feel free to keep me posted on the outcomes."

—————————— 🐾 —

"Stop asking me to reply to this!"

"I apologize for the delay. This has been a particularly busy week but I promise to have an update by (insert date/time). Does this work for you?"

— 🐾 ——————

"This email chain is never-ending!"

"Just doing a quick pulse check—can we find a way to tie this up?"

———————  —

"Why is this email so long?"

"Would you mind highlighting the key points for easier review?"

———————— ✦ ————————

Chapter 3

MEETINGS,
meetings & Zzzz...

🔍 How do I professionally say stop talking so much 🎤

"This meeting could have been an email."

"It seems we're going through some routine updates. Should we think about sending these out via email in the future?

———————— 🔖 —

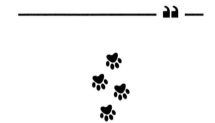

"I don't see why we're discussing this again."

"We seem to be revisiting old ground. Perhaps we can summarize what we've already decided and move forward from there?

— 66 ————————

"Stop talking so much!"

"Let's ensure everyone has a chance to share their thoughts—maybe we can have a quick round of input?"

——————— 🗨 —

"Who decided to schedule this meeting at lunch?"

"I'm wondering if we could avoid lunchtime meetings in the future—lunch is sacred! ;)

— 🗨 ———————

"I don't think we'll ever agree on this."

"It appears we have different viewpoints—maybe we should table this for now and gather more data?"

"Can we skip the small talk and get to it?

Good to catch up with everyone. Now, let's dive into today's agenda.

"Are we seriously having a meeting to decide when to have more meetings?

"It's great to be organized! Let's wrap this up quickly so we can all get back to our tasks - what's the best time for everyone?"

——————————— 🥾 —

"This meeting is pointless."

"I believe we've covered the key points already. Shall we focus on actionable items and follow up later as needed?"

— 🥾 ———————————

"You're just repeating what I said."

"I hear you echoing similar ideas—maybe we can build on what we've both contributed?"

"This discussion is never-ending."

"Let's set a timer to keep our discussions concise and ensure we stay on track."

"Do we really need to discuss every detail?"

"Let's streamline some of these details and focus on the key decisions that need to be made."

———————————— 🙶 —

"I've heard enough about this already."

"I'd love to hear some fresh perspectives—can anyone share new insights on this?"

— 🙶 ————————————

"This meeting could use some caffeine."

"Perhaps a quick coffee break would fuel some fresh ideas?"

———————————— ♪♪ —

"I can't keep up with all these ideas!"

"We have a lot of creative thoughts bouncing around—should we capture them in a shared document?"

— 66 ————————————

"Are you seriously watching Yotube videos while we're talking?"

"I see some screen shenanigans happening! Let's channel that energy into our meeting."

"Can we please stick to the agenda?"

"We seem to be veering off track—let's refer back to our agenda to guide our discussion."

"This is way too many meetings!"

"It feels like we have a lot of meetings—how about we consolidate some of these discussions?"

"This meeting feels like a waste of my time."

"I want to ensure we're all getting value from our discussions—let's check in on our objectives."

"Is that seriously snoring I hear?! This isn't nap time!"

"If anyone needs a break, feel free to grab a coffee and join us! I know meetings can run long."

———————————— 🐾 —

"Is anyone else as confused as I am?"

"I'd love some clarification on this— does anyone else need a recap?"

————————— ✪ —————————

Chapter 4

BUDGET BANTER
Making Cents Of It All

Q How do I ask for a bonus for my performance? 🎤

"This salary offer is way too low."

"I appreciate the offer! Based on my experience and industry standards, I was expecting something in the range of [desired salary]."

———————— 🙶 —

"I can't believe I'm expected to do this for free."

"Could we discuss how this task fits into my current workload and whether it warrants additional compensation?"

— 🙶 ————————

"I deserve a bonus for my performance."

"Considering the impact of my recent contributions, is there room to discuss performance-based incentives?"

———————————— 🔖 —

"You need to give me more budget for this project."

"To ensure the success of this project, I'd like to discuss the possibility of increasing the budget to meet our goals."

— 🔖 ——————————

“I can’t believe you expect me to cover this expense.”

“Could you please clarify the policy on covering expenses related to this project?”

“I’m done doing this for the same pay.”

“I need guidance on how to approach salary discussions within our company. Given the increased responsibilities, I’d like to revisit my compensation structure.”

"If I don't get a raise, I'm going to start job hunting."

"I'd like to discuss my future with the company, including potential opportunities for salary growth."

———————————— 🙙 —

"I can't believe you're asking for a budget cut."

"I'd like to understand the rationale behind the budget reductions and discuss how we can maintain project quality."

— 🙜 ————————

"I can't tell if that thing in the break room is coffee or a science experiment gone wrong."

"Can we explore upgrading our tea and coffee collection? A great brew is essential for a productive day."

—————————— 🙶 —

"This project is underfunded."

"I believe we should revisit the project budget to ensure we have the necessary resources for success."

— 🙶 ——————————

"Stop throwing money at this project without a plan."

"I believe we should develop a clearer financial strategy to guide our spending on this project."

———————— 🙷 —

"No more free food? Seriously?!"

"Could we consider reinstating some form of complimentary food options? It greatly contributes to our workplace culture."

— 🙶 —————————

"Why do I always get the short end of the stick?"

"I'd like to discuss how project allocations can be more equitable moving forward."

"I'm not working overtime for free."

"Could we discuss how overtime hours are compensated to ensure fair recognition of additional effort?"

"How is this company so cheap?"

"I'd like to discuss how our compensation packages can better reflect the market standards."

—————————— ❞ —

"This bonus is laughable."

"Thank you for the bonus! I appreciate the gesture. I would love an opportunity to discuss how we can fine-tune future bonuses to match my ongoing impact."

— ❝ ——————

"Can't we just expense this?"

"Would it be possible to cover this cost as a business expense, given its relevance to the project?"

————————————— 🐾 —

"Stop giving me the runaround with my salary."

"Could you clarify the process for salary adjustments? I'd like to understand how decisions are made."

— 🐾 —————————————

"If you can't pay me more, at least give me more vacation time."

"If an increase in salary isn't feasible right now, I'd love to explore other forms of compensation, such as additional vacation time."

"I can't afford to work here anymore."

"I'd like to discuss my compensation to ensure it meets my financial needs and market standards."

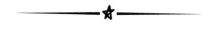

Chapter 5

HOW TO SAY NO
and still look helpful

🔍 How do I politely say this is not my f**** problem! 🎤

"No, I'm not helping with that."

"I'm currently stretched thin, but I can offer guidance on how to proceed if needed."

———————————— ᠈᠈ —

"No, I can't drop everything for your task.

"I'm currently focused on another project, but I can look into this later. Would that work for your timeline?"

— ᠁ ——————————

"I don't do after-work meetings, period!"

"I appreciate the invitation, but I prefer to keep my professional conversations within the office. Let's connect during business hours!"

"Stop asking me for updates!"

"I'm working on this and will provide an update as soon as I have something concrete."

"I don't want to join this meeting."

"I may not be the best person to contribute, but I can review the notes and provide input afterward."

———————— 🐾 —

"This is not my problem."

"I'd be happy to help, though this might be better handled by someone with more expertise in that area."

— 🐾 ————————

"I'm not working on the weekend for this."

"Unfortunately, I'm not available over the weekend, but I can prioritize this first thing Monday."

"I don't think this is necessary."

"I'm wondering if this is essential for the current project goals—what are your thoughts?"

"I'm not answering calls after hours."

"I'm unavailable after 6 PM, but feel free to leave a message, and I'll respond first thing in the morning."

———————— 🥮 —

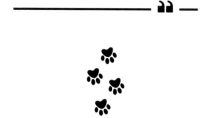

"I don't want to keep going over this."

"I believe we've covered all the major points—can we move forward with the current plan?"

— 🥮 ————————

"I can't take on someone else's work."

"I'm unable to take on extra work at the moment, but I can help brainstorm solutions to move this forward."

"I'm not your assistant."

Can we revisit our responsibilities to ensure we're both aligned and supporting each other's work?

"Your dog is causing chaos, s/he is no longer allowed at work."

"I appreciate your companionship with your pet, but we must maintain our office policy regarding animals for everyone's comfort."

"I'm not signing off on this."

"I'm not comfortable approving this as it stands—let's make some adjustments first."

"Why don't you just do it?"

"Since you're familiar with this, it might be better if you take the lead, but I can assist if needed."

———————————— 🙶 —

"Stop involving me in every decision."

"I trust the team's judgment on this, but feel free to loop me in for key milestones."

— 🙶 ————————————

"Don't expect me to finish this by tomorrow."

"Given the current workload, it's unlikely I'll have this completed by tomorrow, but I can update you on my progress."

"This isn't a priority for me."

"My current priorities are focused on other tasks, but I'm open to discussing how we can align timelines."

"This project isn't worth the effort."

"This project may not align with our top priorities right now—could we discuss its relevance?"

"I'm not dealing with this drama."

"I see this topic is stirring up strong opinions—let's take a breather and come back to it with clearer heads."

Chapter 6

AND FINALLY

when all else fails...

🔍   What is the purpose of life?

AND FINALLY

WHEN ALL ELSE FAILS...

There is always a
well-timed bathroom break!

Desperate times
call for desperate measures.

From the Author

And there you have it—your survival guide to navigating office life without ruffling too many feathers.

As you close this book and head back into the wilds of office life, keep this in mind: the true art of communication is making it through the day without accidentally saying what you're really thinking.

Good luck, and may the HR gods be ever in your favor. Now, if you'll excuse me, I've got some emails to politely ignore.

I am, after all, Still M. Ployed.

⎯⎯⎯⎯⎯✮⎯⎯⎯⎯⎯

If this book made you chuckle—or at least didn't put you to sleep— please drop a review on Amazon. I promise I won't 'follow up' or 'touch base'—just genuine thanks!

Made in United States
North Haven, CT
19 December 2024

62846199R00041